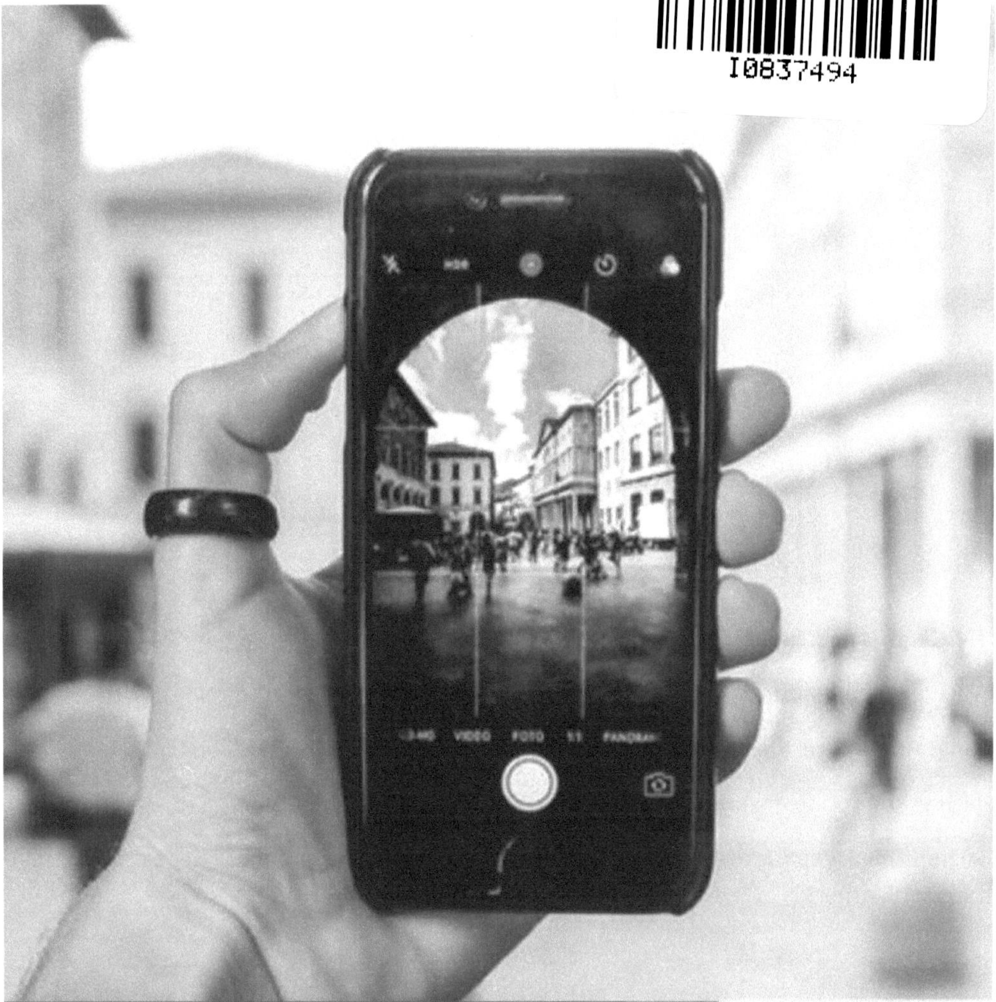

89 Instagram Tips

MostlyBlogging.com

This book is dedicated to my family.

Wayne: I wouldn't be a writer without your support and sacrifice.

Dana: Your interest in my writing career motivated me to publish this book.

Hayley: Your pride encouraged me to continue on my writing journey.

Rachel: Thank you for teaching me about Instagram so I can share these Instagram tips and tricks with others.

–

Instagram tips and tricks.

Why do you need them?

Instagram has everything you could want in a social media site:

High engagement

Ease of generating genuine followers

Feeling of community

Exposure to one billion people

A creative outlet

Opportunities for website traffic

Opportunities for sales.

If you're going to put your energies into generating traffic and sales, why not put your energies where your audience is and your customers are?

Are they on Instagram?

One billion people use Instagram. Everyone is there.

It gets better: Facebook owns Instagram. When you use Instagram, your reach becomes extended across two social media platforms. When I make offers or advertise on Instagram, people looking at my Facebook page will see it.

I went to Instagram looking for traffic and income.

I found a playground.

On Instagram, you can show your followers your playful side.

Let them see your back story without ruining the consistency of the content in your niche on your blog.

You, too, can find belonging, creativity, a place to play and promote your blog, and the highest engagement of any social media site on the Internet.

How?

Just follow these Instagram Tips and Tricks.

By the time you're done reading this complete Instagram guide, you'll know

How to make an Instagram account

How to make posts with engaging Instagram content

How to write Instagram captions that hook your followers

How to make Instagram Stories and Highlights and why you should

How to use IGTV

How to use free Instagram tools for different purposes

Instagram tips and tricks to get targeted followers

Instagram tips and tricks to boost engagement

How to find Instagram groups and DM groups

The value of Whitelists

How to avoid Instagram penalties

How to use Instagram to make money and minimize the competition

Instagram tips and tricks from experts

Let's dive into the Instagram tips and tricks that will help you be successful on Instagram, the most popular social media site on the web.

According to the **DrumUp blog**, "Brand engagement on Instagram is 10X that on Facebook, 54X that on Pinterest and 84X that on Twitter."

Many people are skeptical about whether you can generate enough interest on Instagram to see website traffic and make sales on Instagram.

Consider these comments from blogger **Antony Angel**:

"I'm trying to grow my Instagram following but the platform is designed in such that, only if you shell out enough money on sponsored posts, research, analytics, and influencer marketing, can you get some actionable results and a wider reach."

This post should put such reservations to rest. By the time you're done reading this post, you'll see how you can generate a following on Instagram and monetize your Instagram account.

89 of the Best Mostly-Free Instagram Tips and Tricks

How to make an Instagram account

Creating a business profile is free and easy.

Tip 1: Use your phone. Instagram was designed to be used with the Instagram app.

Tip 2: When you sign up, ask for an Instagram business account. Scroll down to Create Business Profile. Make sure you have a public account and not a private one or you won't be able to select this option.

Business accounts come with insightful analytics. Also, in late 2018, Instagram changed its algorithm. Supposedly, this change favored business accounts. Business accounts are free. Having an Instagram business account is to your benefit. There is no downside.

Tip 3: Type in your email address. When people click my profile picture, they will see the word "Email" which is a live link. Clicking will enable people to email me. This is great if people want to hire me for blog coaching or a sponsored post.

Tip 4: Import your Facebook followers. Many of your Facebook friends already use Instagram. By exporting them, you can connect immediately and start with a higher follower count.

Tip 5: Consider Instagram's suggestions for who to follow.

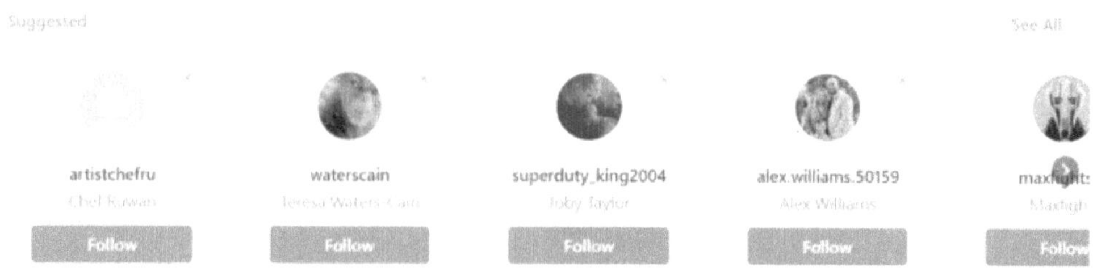

You will see these suggestions on both your computer and the Instagram app.

Tip 6: Do not follow people without a profile picture. Look at the first suggestion. Why not? People without a profile picture aren't that active.

Tip 7: Be selective in who you follow. Instagram only allows you to follow 7,500 people.

Instagram Profile

Your bio is pivotal to getting the attention of other Instagrammers. The first thing they'll check out is your bio and in a moment decide if they want to follow you.

Tip 8: Write the best bio you can. Your profile is like your online business card. The characters are limited so make good use of them. I am constantly tweaking my bio.

Janice Wald 💻 Blogging
⭐Tips for online success
⭐Tips for bloggers of all levels
⭐Entrepreneur quotes
⭐Featured in @Huffpost
⭐Grab your free resources below 🔽
linktr.ee/janicewald

Tip 9: Use emojis. They are eye-catching. When you go to your profile in the Instagram app, click edit. This will bring up the emoji icon to the left of the space bar.

Tip 10: Include your email in your bio so people can reach you. If you have a business account, Instagram's analytics will tell you how many people click your email link each week.

Tip 11: Choose a profile picture that reflects what you do.

When you see me on my iPad, there is no question that my niche, the content my Instagram posts will center around, is content creation on the web. Between the computer emoji and watching me type on my iPad, the type of Instagram content you'll see on my Instagram account is pretty clear.

I actually can't take credit. I first got the idea from famed blogger **Yaro Starak**.

Tip 12: Put your main hashtag in your Instagram profile. Notice mine says "blogging."

Tip 13: In your Instagram profile, offer people something for free. Look at the last line in my profile: "Grab your free resources below" and the arrow points to my free resources in my Linktree link.

Tip 14: Make a LinkTree account. You're only allowed ONE link in your Instagram profile. Which will you pick? Why not pick them all?

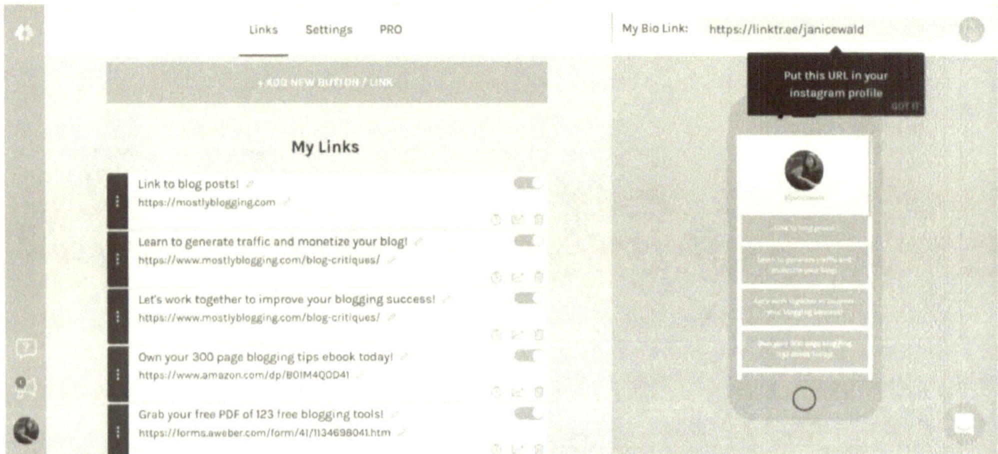

By making a LinkTree account, you're able to link your post links together and list them at LinkTree. When people click your LinkTree link, they'll be taken to as many links as you have there. I don't know the maximum number, but I haven't encountered it yet, and I've been there a while.

How to make posts with engaging Instagram content

How To Become
A Successful
Business Woman
LADYBOSSBLOGGER.COM

Image Credit: https://www.instagram.com/ladybossblogger/?hl=en

Tip 15: Choose a pattern you want your Instagram content to follow. Many people choose checkerboard. Will you?

Tip 16: Faces do well on Instagram. (Source: Helene in Between**)**

Tip: 17. I read the color blue does well on Instagram.

Tip: 18. Make Instagram content with a complimentary color scheme. Choose a color palette and stick to it.

Tip: 19. Use the Preview app to make sure your Instagram content compliments each other. Preview is free.

[caption id="attachment_31782" align="aligncenter" width="700"]

Flatlay styling for Instagram.

ing on with, be sure to check out Later's New Instagram Features in 2018 post which take

Image Credit: https://marketingvision.co.uk/]

Tip 20: The Marketing Vision blog recommends shooting your Instagram photos from above the subject of the photo.

Tip 21: Try to make your feed look different from others in your niche. As people scroll, your Instagram content will catch their eye if it looks different.

Tip 22: Post videos. Anthony Groeper explains you have a better chance of being chosen for the Explore Section, the section that's shown to the majority of Instagram users. Anthony explains the reason: If you watch a video, you'll stay on Instagram's site longer.

Tip 23: Post Instagram content a maximum of 4 times a day. I've read fewer numbers but never more than 4.

Tip 24: Post consistently. You don't want to confuse your readers.

Tip 25: Be consistent when using filters. Your Instagram feed should look like an art gallery, not a jumble of filters. Would you like to see **my Instagram feed**? At Instagram, go to @janicewald

If you look at my feed, you see a great deal of consistency:

I use blue and colors that complement blue.

My niche, blogging, doesn't lend itself to visuals. No problem!

As someone who tries to inspire people in their online journey, I have inspirational quotes with pictures that match.

Do you recall I recommended using faces? Look at all the faces in my Instagram photos!

Tip 26: Find a "buddy" in your niche. Share your content with each other. When you tag your "buddy," their followers will see your content and vice versa. You both end up expanding your reach. Your "buddy" should have roughly the same number of followers as you do.

Tip 27: Choose pictures that evoke emotion. Emotions make people take action, actions like visiting your blog, following your blog, and buying from you.

How to Write Instagram Captions

How long should your Instagram caption be?

I've heard mixed. Some people put their entire blog post into their caption!

Other people advise keeping your caption short.

Tip 28: Vary the length. Then see which Instagram content gets the best engagement from your followers.

Tip 29: Start your caption with a question. Questions are engaging. They make great hooks. Try to ask a question which will elicit at least a four-word answer. Why? The more comments the first hour, the greater the chance you'll be chosen for the Explorer Section and receive mass exposure. However, if your comments are less than four words long, Instagram doesn't consider them.

Tip 30: Tell a relatable story in your caption. Stories also make great hooks.

Tip 31: Use inspirational quotes in your captions and Instagram posts. The Instagram crowd loves inspirational quotes. You can find the quotes anywhere: Pinterest, Tumblr, or Google are good places to start.

Tip 32: Use 30 hashtags. Someone compared hashtags to lottery tickets. You're given 30. Use them!

Tip 33: Make sure your hashtags are relevant to your Instagram content. How? I recommend <u>All-Hashtags</u>. You type in your focus word, and it generates 30 hashtags. You have your choice of Top or Random hashtags.

Tip 34: Vary the popularity of your hashtags. Some people advise against using only <u>popular hashtags</u>. If you do, your Instagram content could get lost in the crowd.

Tip 35: Use the Geotag option. When you tag your location, I've heard you have a greater chance of getting into the Explore Section. The Explore Section is shown to so many Instagrammers, you'll experience tremendous growth if you're selected for the section.

Tip 36: Use <u>Best 9</u> (https://2017bestnine.com/) and duplicate the kind of Instagram content that resonates with your followers.

These are my best 9, the Instagram content my followers engaged with the most in 2018.

Tip 37: Use your own name as a hashtag. Your name becomes more recognizable so this strategy boosts your brand awareness.

Tip 38: Put your signature hashtag last in your caption. Then, it functions as your signature. in other words, the last hashtag in my caption is #MostlyBlogging.

Tip 39: Include a Call to Action in your caption. What do you want them to do? Click the live link in your bio? Click the like button? Leave a comment? Share your Instagram content? Buy your product or service?

Tip 40: Ask people to tag 3 friends. This way, your post will get shared and you'll expand your exposure.

Tip 41: Post your Instagram content according to the following schedule: When people are going to bed, just getting to work, or checking out to return home for the day, they're most likely to be checking their Instagram feed according to **<u>research conducted by CoSchedule</u>**.

Instagram Stories and Instagram Highlights

Tip 42: Use Instagram Stories

What is an Instagram Story?

The site has a feature called "Stories." Stories only sit at the top of Instagram for 24 hours. Everyone who follows you will only see your content for 24 hours. These stories are prominently displayed at the top of all your followers' Instagram feed and will stay there until the 24 hours elapse.

Although your "story" goes away in 24 hours, you will be able to see in real-time how many people have seen your image or video.

Instagram Stories allow your creativity and playful side to come out.

Tip 43: Put videos into your Instagram Story.

How to save a video to your "story."

By saving a video to your story, it will sit on top of your followers' feed for 24 hours.

1. **Open your Instagram app on your mobile device.**
2. **Swipe right. This will activate the camera.**
3. **Hold the big white button in for a video.** Let go of the button when you're done with the video.
4. **Tap the video when you're done.**
5. **Click the Aa for the font.** You can type and change the colors.
6. **Swipe either right or left for filters.**
7. **Swipe up for emojis. You can change the size.**
8. **Tilt anything you've added by pinching the element.**
9. **If you wish to save your video, click "Save" at the bottom of the screen.**
10. **Choose who you wish to share with.** If you want your video at the top of your Instagram feed, click "Your Story." Everyone will be able to see. If you want to share with individuals, click "Next" and choose those individuals from your contacts.

Tip 44: Put still images in your Instagram Story. Many free tools come with <u>free stock images</u> as an option to using your own photos.

Tip 45: Include Emojis. They're engaging.

Tip 46: Use hashtags. You're allowed one hashtag in an Instagram Story.

Tip 47: Include the CTA, "Swipe Up", if you have more than 10,000 followers. That link is gold. It can take people who see your Instagram Story anywhere you want-- your optin form, your product's Amazon sale page, or a relevant article you're trying to boost traffic to, for example.

Tip 48: Use the Storeo app. Since Instagram videos can only be 15 seconds long, the Storeo app will break your video into pieces for you. Just upload them to your Instagram Stories one at a time.

Tip 49: Use Instagram Story templates. Canva, Typorama, PixTeller, Spark Post app, and PosterMyWall are examples of tools you can use to make Instagram Story.

Tip 50: Put your Instagram Story into a highlight. Your Instagram content will stay in your highlights and not disappear like your other Instagram Stories after 24 hours.

Tip 51: Have polls. You'll get feedback on your blog post ideas.

Tip 52: Ask questions. You'll engage your followers.

Tip 53: Use IGTV. To use IGTV, you need an app. When you make your live videos (as well as recorded videos), make sure you hold your phone vertically. You need portrait orientation. You're allowed to link to your IGTV in your Instagram Story whether or not you have 10,000 followers. You can save your IGTV in your Highlights and link to your IGTV in your Stories.

Tip 54: Use Collages.

Using collages in your Instagram Stories (and in your feed) accomplishes several purposes.

I made this collage using the Unfold app.

This is free advertising for me. Making a Story is free, so it costs me nothing to market my books.

Next, your Instagram feed and Story looks different from others when you use collages, further drawing attention to your brand.

Tip 55: Use the Slider Option in your Stories.

Look:

Do you see how I used a poll? There were only two choices-- Yes or No.

What if I asked a question that required degrees of response, for example, Agree, Strongly Agree, Disagree, etc?

The poll option only allows two choices. However, the Slider option allows the follower to slide the slider to show where on the spectrum they agree or disagree.

Go to the GIF feature and select Slider. If you don't see it, type Slider into search.

When it comes up, type your question.

The Slider is extremely engaging. When your follower slides it to the right, the face on the Slider gets bigger. When they vote, a heart flies into the air.

Also, like with the poll, you get feedback from your community that will help you make decisions regarding future website content. For example, I asked how comfortable people are making videos. If everyone answers, "Extremely comfortable" on the Slider, there's little point in composing articles that will tell my readers how to become more comfortable.

I linked to my blog post article telling people how to **make videos**. I never waste the opportunity to link! Always get in your call to action! Do you see my Call to Action in red on the right?

Instagram Tools

Tip 56: Use tools for making Instagram quote posts. These perform well on Instagram.

Tip 57: When you make them, use relevant quote hashtags so everyone looking for quotes can find your Instagram content.

Tip 58: Use tools which show you your Instagram analytics. For example, SocialBakers.com is a free tool which will show you your most liked and commented on posts. Knowing this information will enable you to replicate this content to achieve the same kind of interest from your audience in the future.

Instagram Tips and Tricks to Get Followers

Tip 59: Go to LinkedIn and type Instagram into the search bar. Follow people who work for Instagram on LinkedIn. When choosing Instagram content for the Explore section, the powers-that-be may remember you from LinkedIn.

How to get targeted followers on Instagram

Tip 60: Go to the Explore Section. Like and comment. Instagram shows you the kind of posts you have a history of liking.

Tip 61: Type your #niche into the Search bar to find people who create the kind of Instagram content you create. They'll be interested in your content and likely follow you. You can search by Top Posts or Most Recent.

Tip 62: Follow 30 people an hour depending on your availability. If they're in your niche, they'll likely follow you back.

How to boost Instagram engagement

Tip 63: Comment on other people's Instagram content.

Then, they'll be the more likely comment on your posts.

Tip 64: Like other people's Instagram content.

Then, they'll be more likely to like your posts.

Also, if you don't comment and like, people will consider you a "ghost follower." There are tools Instagrammers use to detect and unfollow ghost followers.

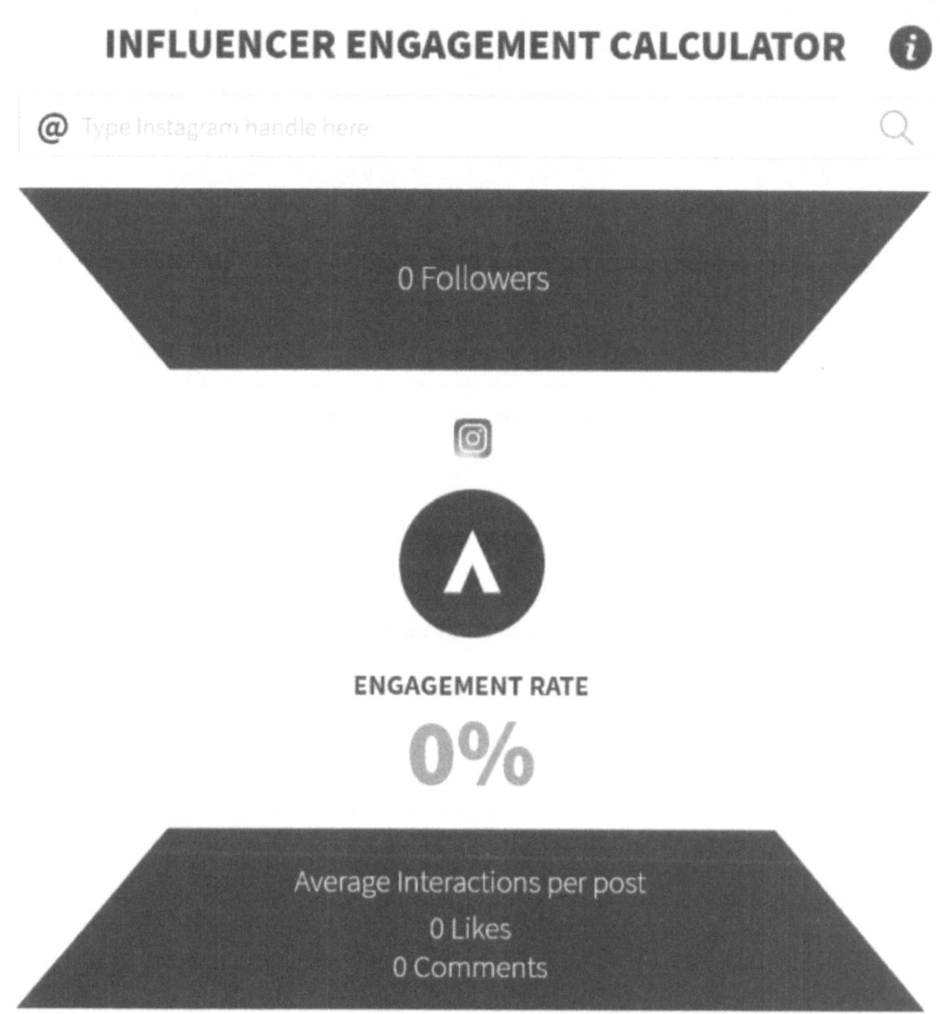

Tip 65: Use the <u>Instagram Calculator</u> to ensure you are engaging enough. If not, step up your game! That way your followers will reciprocate and engage more with you.

Tip 66: Return people's comments. This way, people will be compelled to return your comments.

Tip 67: Return people's comments within the first hour of posting. I heard if people get a great many likes and comments within the first hour of publication, they have a greater chance of being in the Explorer Section.

Tip 68: Include CTA's (Call to Actions) in your captions. Ask people to like, comment, and share your Instagram content.

Tip 69: Host giveaways. People love giveaways and they are a great way to boost engagement. For example, will you randomly draw from people who commented or shared? When they share, make sure they use the hashtag associated with your giveaway. Then, all you need to do is type that hashtag into the search bar to find the shares.

Tip 70: Share other people's posts with your Instagram followers. You can easily do this with the free Regrammer app.

Join Engagement Groups and DM Groups

Tip 71: Join Instagram Engagement Groups and Follow Loops.

What is an Engagement Group?

Instagram Engagement groups can be found anywhere: Facebook, Instagram, the Telegram app, Snapchat...

The goal of the group is to boost your comments, likes, and follows.

What is a Follow Loop?

In the Instagram search bar, type #FollowLoop or #FollowTrain. You will find groups looking to grow their following. Follow trains effectively and quickly grow your follower count.

Tip 72: Join an Instagram DM Group

What is a DM Group?

DM Groups are like Engagement Groups. The purpose is the same. **The difference:** DM groups are only on Instagram.

I've also heard Engagement Groups called "DM Groups" since people in the groups communicate through the Direct Message feature.

According to **Anthony Groeper**, joining a DM group will make your account go viral.

He belongs to 500 groups! He recommends belonging to at least 100 if you want a chance to land in the Explore Section, the section with the most exposure on Instagram.

His strategy: If you send your post 240 times a day to different groups, your account will go viral.

Note: You must be invited to join these groups.

Membership in engagement groups are so sought after, I've heard of people pay hundreds of dollars to get in!

I've personally never paid to join an Engagement group. Luckily, people in my groups were forming new groups and invited me to join.

If you go to Instagram, and type #DMGroups into the search bar, you'll see people looking for DM Group members.

You can also try forming your own group. Group admins often ask a lot of their members so you get leverage if you have your own group. For example, many groups require members to follow their accounts.

Unfollowing people

Although you can only follow 30 people per hour, Instagram allows you to unfollow 160 people per hour.

Why would you want to unfollow people on Instagram?

You won't be allowed to continue to follow people in your niche if you reach 7500 followers.

You need to follow people whose content might interest you and whose content makers might follow you back.

You need to unfollow people you've changed your mind about, people who don't return your follow, or inactive followers.

Tip 73: Be patient. Instagram followers accumulate by snowballing. When people see your Instagram follower count is higher than others, the Bandwagon Effect comes into play. People assume if others are following your account, it must be good, and they should follow you as well.

Have White Lists

Tip 74: Have a White List

What is an Instagram White List?

Let me explain.

Suppose you want to follow someone who doesn't follow you back?

This happened to me. I joined and Instagram Engagement group. The requirement was I had to follow the admin of the group. He didn't follow me back. My Unfollow tool will unfollow him unless I put him on a White List. People on a White List won't be unfollowed.

The InstaUnfollow app has a White List that costs $11.00 for the year. You can also pay per month.

How to avoid getting shadowbanned:

Tip 75: Follow the Instagram rules. Follow a maximum of 30 people per hour and unfollow a maximum of 160 people per hour.

Tip 76: Don't duplicate hashtags. Have various hashtag groups ready to copy-paste. I have a group for my SEO captions, a group for my blogging tips captions, a group for my social media captions, and so forth. Preparing them in groups of 30 ahead of time will save you a great deal of time when you're rushing to post on Instagram.

Tip 77: Don't buy followers. It's been rumored that Instagram is cracking down on buying followers.

How to Make Money with Instagram

Are you aware you can use the power of Instagram to market your products and services? Instagram marketing is easy, free, and quick. Instagram marketing is also a common form of advertising.

Don't believe me? I typed #offers in the Instagram search bar and 451,390 offers came up. Don't worry, by the end of this post, we will have you beating the competition for consumer attention.

Once you're able to generate targeted followers, you can actually monetize your Instagram followers.

Tip 78: Put your website link and your contact link in your profile. This way, potential customers can contact you.

Tip 79: Advertise your products and services in your Instagram Stories. People will rush to click knowing the offer is time-sensitive since stories vanish 24 hours after posting.

See Tip 54. With one Instagram story, I advertised two of my books using a template from the Unfold app.

Did anyone answer my Call to Action and click within the 24-hour window the Story was visible?

Look:

You may feel 5 clicks in 24 hours isn't a large number. However, remember I was selling two books with each click. I could have potentially sold 10 books that day without spending a penny on advertising.

Did this method work? Did I make any money selling ebooks during that 24-hour period?

Yes! Look:

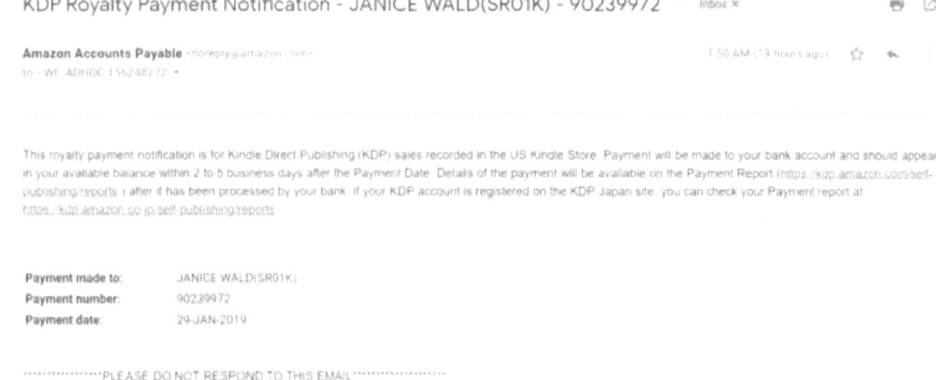

Note: I made money quickly and easily without needing an advertising budget or blog traffic, and now you can too.

Tip 80: Minimize your competition for sales. Type what you are advertising offers about into the Instagram search bar. To figure out the number of photos posted on a specific hashtag, simply type the word you'd like to use as a hashtag into the search bar on Instagram. Then check the number under the hashtag. This number tells you how many photos using this hashtag are currently on Instagram. The fewer the number, the less competition you have.

Tip 81: Make ads displaying your products or ads of consumers using your products happily. One of the perks of having a business account is you'll be able to create an ad. However, you have to pay to promote your content.

Tip 82: Engage your followers by having them post pictures of your products or videos of them using your products.

Tip 83: Make sure the photos you post are so visually appealing, they grab users' attention.

Tip 84: Share special promotions or coupons.

Tip 85: Get your followers involved in a contest and turn those leads into email signups you can eventually market to.

Tip 86: Use Instagram's shoppable posts. This will cost you, but it's a way to sell on Instagram.

Tip 87: Be patient. People give their money to people they trust. Generating trust takes time.

Tip 88: Sign up for <u>AmbassadHer</u>. It costs $2.99 a month, but you should make it back when brands hire you. For example, I've already been approached from the AmbassadHer company about working with Tide. They offered to give me a reward worth $30 if I bought Tide pods and showed a photo on Instagram and put a link to the company in my bio for 2 weeks. I turned it down, but that's the kind of offer I received.

It gets better: You see the offers for free. You don't spend any money unless you apply for the gig.

Tip 89: Sign up for <u>Valued Voice</u>. Problogger <u>Deborah</u> received the most work from this company in the past, she reports.

Experts Share Their Best Instagram Tips and Tricks

I asked two experts, "What are your best Instagram tips and tricks?"

1. Nirav Dave <u>Capsicum Mediaworks</u>

To make an impact on Instagram you need to, first, know who your target audience is. By researching and finding out your target audience, you'll be able to come up with a strategy that aligns with your brand and caters to the need of your target audience. Three effective tips to use are

Share Beautiful and Optimized Images: Instagram is all about stunning visuals. As such, you need to ensure that the images you post are not only high-quality but they are also optimized to improve engagement. Be creative with your images but ensure that it has a consistent look, in terms of grid layout and theme.

Compose a Compelling Caption: A stunning image accompanied by a well-written caption can go a long way in engaging your audience and will get you more like and comments. Just ensure to keep it brief and relevant.

Make Use of Trending Hashtags: To find the trendiest hashtags for your Instagram post, use the Ritetag chrome extension. This tool provides you with relevant hashtag suggestions for text as well as images.

2. Chiranjeevi Maddala <u>Digital Ready</u>

Below are some of the tips that the audience can use for Instagram.

1) **Stay updated** on **all the latest features that Instagram introduces.** Make use of those trends to increase audience engagement as well as followers. Following the latest trends shows your audience that you are an up-to-date brand, aware of all the new-age trends.

2) **Make your posts creative.** Photoshop doesn't work every time. Infuse creativity in your posts, Include real people, engage concepts, Q&A videos and anything else that you think can positively attract the audience.

3) **Avoid a shadow ban.** One of the things that can greatly affect your Instagram account is a shadowban. Shadowban refers to the condition where your hashtags get undiscoverable. This leads to a lower engagement on your Instagram posts. While this is a temporary situation, you can avoid getting your posts shadowbanned in a number of ways, such as
- Slowing down your posts for a couple of days
- Use mixed up hashtags. Don't use the same hashtags for a long period of time
- Don't use bots for automated liking or commenting

Wrapping Up: A Guide to Instagram Tips and Tricks

In closing, Instagram offers marketers a great deal of potential. Considering the site is gaining in popularity, that potential is on the rise.

When surveyed, 60% of consumers reported finding new products on Instagram. One-third of the Stories viewed are from businesses. According to **statistics**, over 1 million companies advertise on this popular site. Now that you know these tips, so can you.

Have you tried to boost your Instagram game?

I have.

While trying to learn the ropes, I encountered conflicting information.

When I attempted to research Instagram tips and tricks, there seemed to be a lack of definitive answers. Hopefully, this guide brought clarity.

To be a successful marketer, you need to go where your audience goes. Since one billion people are going to Instagram, you should go there too. What are you waiting for?

For more Instagram tips and tricks, subscribe to MostlyBlogging.com.

www.ingramcontent.com/pod-product-compliance
Lightning Source LLC
Chambersburg PA
CBHW051143250726
18655CB00007B/3208